Lost
Football Le...
Grounds
From The Air

Lost
Football League
Grounds
From The Air

Aerofilms

Ian Allan
PUBLISHING

First published 2005

ISBN (10) 0 7110 3080 4
ISBN (13) 978 0 7110 3080 0

Text © Ian Allan Publishing 2005
Photographs © Simmons Aerofilms 2005

Published by Ian Allan Publishing

an imprint of Ian Allan Publishing Ltd, Hersham, Surrey KT12 4RG.

Printed by Ian Allan Printing Ltd, Hersham, Surrey KT12 4RG.

Code: 0508/B3

Visit the Ian Allan Publishing web site at www.ianallanpublishing.com

Front cover:
Maine Road — Manchester City,
see page 64.
1 May 1997 666121

Half title:
Highfield Road — Coventry, see page 54.
26 May 2001 688710

Frontispiece:
Leeds Road — Huddersfield, see page 62.
July 1934 45323

Aerofilms

Aerofilms was founded in 1919 and has specialised in the acquisition of aerial photography within
the United Kingdom throughout its history. The company has a record of being innovative in the
uses and applications of aerial photography.

Photographs looking at the environment in perspective are called oblique aerial photographs.
These are taken with Hasselblad cameras by professional photographers experienced in the difficult
conditions encountered in aerial work.

Photographs taken straight down at the landscape are termed vertical aerial photographs. These
photographs are obtained using Leica survey cameras, the products from which are normally used in
the making of maps.

Aerofilms has a unique library of oblique and vertical photographs in excess of one and a half
million in number covering the United Kingdom. This library of photographs dates from 1919 to the
present day and is being continually updated.

Oblique and vertical photography can be taken to customers' specification by Aerofilms'
professional photographers.

To discover more of the wealth of past or present photographs held in the library at Aerofilms or
to commission new aerial photographs, please contact:

Simmons Aerofilms, 32-34 Station Close, Potters Bar, Herts EN6 1TL.
Telephone: 01707 648390   Fax: 01707 648399
Web-site: www.simmonsaerofilms.com   E-mail: info@aerofilms.com

Contents

Introduction 6
Arsenal Stadium 10
Athletic Ground 12
Ayresome Park 14
Baseball Ground .16
Boothferry Park 18
Borough Park 22
Bower Fold 24
Burnden Park 26
County Ground 28
Dean Court 30
Drill Field 32
Eastville 34
Elm Park 38
Feethams 42
Fellows Park 44
Filbert Street 46
Gay Meadow 48
Goldstone Ground .50
Haig Avenue 52
Highfield Road 54
Holker Street 56
Horsley Hill 58
Lea Bridge Stadium 60
Leeds Road 62
Maine Road 64
Manor Ground 66
Millfields Road 68
National Hockey Stadium 70

Northolme 72
Odsal 74
Old Recreation Ground 76
Old Show Ground .78
Park Avenue 80
Peel Croft 82
Peel Park 84
Penydarren Park 86
Plough Lane 88
Portland Park 90
Recreation Ground 92
Roker Park 94
Sealand Road 96
Seedhill 98
Somerton Park 100
Southend Stadium 102
Springfield Park .104
The Dell 106
The Den 108
The Nest 110
Tower Athletic Ground 112
Twerton Park 114
Vetch Field 116
Victoria Ground .118
Watling Street 120
Wembley 122
West Ham Stadium 124
White City 126
Index of clubs 128

Introduction

Since the Football League was established in 1888 there has been an almost constant change in the teams that competed within it. Partly this was the result of the gradual expansion of the League into the four divisions that existed prior to the creation of the Premiership in 1992 but, even in the years when there was no automatic promotion between the higher non-league divisions and the lowest level of the Football League, teams could and did fail to get re-elected on a regular basis. In the earlier years of the Football League, moreover, clubs came and went with regularity; few today, for example, will recall that places such as Burton upon Trent and Aberdare were once proud hosts of teams in the League.

More than 200 grounds have played host to Football League matches over the years and it does not require a Nobel Prize winning mathematician to work out that, with only 92 clubs forming the top four divisions in England and Wales, there are more than 100 locations where grounds no longer play host to League football. There are a number of factors behind these 'lost' grounds. In some cases, the clubs concerned have relocated, in many cases more than once, over their history; moreover, recent years, as a result of the tragedies at Valley Parade in 1985 and Hillsborough in 1989, have seen a number of clubs construct new, state-of-the-art stadia. This trend will continue with teams such as Arsenal, Liverpool, Milton Keynes and Shrewsbury Town all planning on relocating over the next few years. The 2005/06 season will be the last that Arsenal plays at Highbury before relocating to the new Emirates Stadium that is rapidly rising adjacent to the railway line at Finsbury Park and Shrewsbury Town relocate from the picturesque Gay Meadow alongside the River Severn to the New Meadow on the Oteley Road. Whilst neither of these grounds in technically 'lost' at present, both are included as their fate would appear to be sealed. Other current grounds that may well disappear in the near future include Anfield (Liverpool), Belle Vue (Doncaster Rovers), Layer Road (Colchester United), Roots Hall (Southend United) and York Street (Boston United).

Ayresome Park — Middlesbrough, see page 14.
12 June 1973 259379

Another factor in the disappearance of grounds is the collapse of the teams associated with them. Whilst it is relatively rare for a team to collapse financially during the course of a season, as Accrington Stanley did during the 1961/62 and Aldershot in 1991/92, a number of teams have folded at the end of a season, most recently Maidstone United at the end of 1991/92. Other teams, such as Bradford Park Avenue and Newport County, have ultimately failed after relegation from the Football League and, whilst these clubs — as with Accrington Stanley — may have been subsequently revived, their traditional homes have been lost.

There are also those League grounds belonging to teams which have lost their League status but which have continued to see football at a lower level. Teams such as Workington Town, Barrow and Southport still occupy the grounds that they played at during their League career and, with the enhanced opportunity for promotion to the League as a result of two-up/two-down from the Conference, there is every possibility that at some stage in the future, providing the facilities meet League criteria, these teams could once again reclaim a League status, as teams such as Barnet, Carlisle United, Colchester United, Doncaster Rovers, Lincoln City and Shrewsbury Town have done in recent in recent years. The corollary of this, however, is that two teams will always get relegated boosting the Conference number of 'lost' League Grounds. However, in establishing the criteria for the book, those clubs that have been relegated to the Conference since the advent of automatic promotion and relegation have been excluded as these teams — as shown by clubs such as Doncaster Rovers and Colchester United — can return to the League. Clubs that failed to be re-elected are included on the basis that the grounds that exist today may be significantly different to the grounds that existed when the team actually played in the League.

This project is based around the unique archive that Simmons Aerofilms has built up over the years since the company first took aerial photographs in 1919. By careful research it has proved possible to track down most — but unfortunately — not all grounds that have been lost since that year as well as a few that succumbed earlier.

Baseball Ground — Derby, see page 16.
April 1921 5810

Arsenal Stadium

One of three grounds likely to disappear at the end of the 2005/06 season is perhaps one of the best known and famous grounds in the country — Arsenal's ground at Highbury (as the Arsenal Stadium is more familiarly known). As fans attend games at this historic ground during this final season, they'll be able to see the finishing touches being made to the new Emirates Stadium to the west of the existing ground. Although the site at Highbury has been sold for redevelopment and will be used for housing, this work will incorporate the listed West and East stands and so part of Highbury will survive to remind fans of this traditional home of football. Arsenal played its first game at the newly constructed stadium at Highbury on 6 September 1913. At that stage the ground comprised a Main (East) Stand designed by Archibald Leitch and three open terraces constructed upon spoil removed by the tunnelling for the nearby Piccadilly Line. The next phase of the ground's development occurred in 1932 with the construction of the Claude Ferrier-designed West Stand. Ferrier also designed expanded terraces at both the North and South ends; this work was followed by the provision of a cover over the North End in 1935 — this was destroyed by bombing during World War 2 — and the rebuilding of the East Stand to a design of William Binnie in 1936. Postwar, the cover over the North End was replaced in 1954. In 1989 the Clock (South) End was fitted with executive boxes and a cover, although this roof did not extend over the whole end, leaving some seats, which were installed in 1993 when Highbury was made all-seater, exposed to the elements. Both the East and West stands were refurbished and, in May 1992, the final phase in the redevelopment of the ground occurred with the demolition of the North Bank and its replacement by a new North Stand, which opened on 14 August 1993. With an all-seated capacity of less than 40,000, Highbury was increasingly inadequate for the club's needs but there was little prospect for expansion. Thus the decision was made to relocate to the new ground, which was constructed on a brownfield site in nearby Ashburton Grove.

26 May 2001 688310

Athletic Ground

Between 1921 and 1927, the Athletic Ground — or the Ynys Stadium — played host to League football as Aberdare Athletic was elected to Division Three for the start of the 1921/22 season. The ground had been first used for football in 1893 when Aberdare Town based itself there; Aberdare Athletic itself was formed in 1920 by which date a narrow stand had been constructed on the south side. This was enlarged shortly before the club gained admission to the League when the end terraces were also completed; these replaced part of the cycle track that had previously surrounded the pitch. Unfortunately, Athletic failed to

be re-elected in 1927 and so dropped out of the League and, seven years later, ceased to use the ground. Although the photograph was taken looking towards the northeast some years after the ground was used for League football, it shows to reasonable effect the ground and its environment. The site was subsequently redeveloped as a sports centre.

16 August 1955 R25344

Ayresome Park

Pictured in April 1966, Ayresome Park is seen looking northwestwards with work in progress on covering the East Terrace as part of the programme of ground improvements undertaken before England hosted the World Cup that year. In addition to the cover over the East Terrace, Ayresome Park was also provided with an additional 7,600 seats. When Middlesbrough moved to the ground from the club's previous ground at Linthorpe Road in 1903, the team was already playing League football. Facilities in 1903 included a Main (North) Stand, built to a design by Archibald Leitch, and the grandstand from Linthorpe Road relocated on the south. The original South Stand was rebuilt in 1936-37. Also before World War 2, the Holgate (West) End was provided with a cover. Floodlighting was first installed in 1957. Although there were plans to convert Ayresome Park into an all-seater ground, the take-over of the club by Steve Gibson brought relocation forward and, in July 1994, plans for the new ground were unveiled. Middlesbrough played its last game at the ground on 30 April 1995 before relocating to the Riverside Stadium; the old ground has subsequently been demolished.
29 April 1966 A160783

Baseball Ground

Initially developed in the 1880s by the owner of the adjacent foundry, the ground was used, as its name implies, for baseball after 1889. Although Derby County moved to the ground permanently in 1895, the team had played a number of matches at the Baseball Ground in 1892. The club was already a member of the Football League in 1895. The photograph, taken looking towards the east, portrays the grounds as it existed in 1972. The Main (West) Stand dated from rebuilding work in 1926 and opened in September of that year. On the east was the Popular Side; this had originally been covered in the late 1920s, but in the form illustrated here had been modified in 1969 with the construction of a second tier. Following this work, covers were provided at both the Normanton and Ormaston Ends with the result that, by 1933, the Baseball Ground could offer covered accommodation on all four sides. The ground remained largely unchanged after the 1971 season, with the exception of additional seating, but in 1996, after some uncertainty, it was decided that the club would relocate rather than redevelop the Baseball Ground. The final League match at the Baseball Ground occurred on 11 May 1997 and the club moved to Pride Park for the start of the 1997/98 season. For a number of years the Baseball Ground was retained for reserve team matches, but this later ceased and the ground was demolished during late 2003 and the first part of 2004.
3 July 1972 A242197

Boothferry Park

Although the site for the future Boothferry Park had been acquired as early as 1930, it was not until after World War 2 that the ground was constructed and Hull City, already a member of the Football League, played its first game there on 31 August 1946, having relocated from its earlier ground at Anlaby Road. The ground as constructed consisted of a Main (West) Stand and terracing along with a temporary cover at the North End. The North Stand was constructed in 1950 and, on 6 January 1951, trains first used Boothferry Park Halt on the adjacent railway line. The view here, taken in 1972 looking towards the northwest, shows, in addition to the West Stand and North End, the cover installed on the East Side in 1951 and South Stand constructed in 1965. The floodlights shown were installed in October 1964, replacing equipment originally dating from 1953. Subsequent to the construction of the South Stand, the only work to alter the ground's appearance occurred in 1982 when, after the club went into receivership, the North Stand was demolished to be replaced by a supermarket and a small covered terrace. For the next decade the future of Boothferry Park was uncertain; however, once the local authority had sold its local telephone company and announced that part of the proceeds would be used to fund the construction of a new stadium to be shared by Hull City and Hull RLFC, the writing was on the wall. Hull City played its last football league match at the ground during the 2001/02 season but the old ground is still standing in 2005 awaiting redevelopment.
17 July 1972 A234735

Overleaf:
22 September 1955 R25628

Borough Park

The home of Workington Town from 1937, when it was constructed with the assistance of the local council, Borough Park played host to League football for more than a quarter of a century, from 1951, when the club was elected to Division Three (N), to 1977, when the club failed to be re-elected and was replaced by Wimbledon. As constructed, the ground included a 1,000-seat Main Stand on the west. Terracing was later added, as were covers on the north and south sides as shown in this photograph dating from 1968. The cover on the East (Popular) Side was added in 1956 with the floodlighting being installed the following year. Since the club fell out of the Football League, it has continued to function in the non-league pyramid and Borough Park remains its home. The ground, however, has undergone some changes with the old Main Stand now shorn of its roof and much reduced and the cover over the north end also removed to provide, once again, open terracing.
17 July 1968 A187999

Bower Fold

Stalybridge Celtic, a founder member of Division Three (N) in 1921, was first to play at Bower Fold in 1906. By the time that the club entered the League, the ground comprised a 500-seat East Stand, built shortly after the end of World War 1, and banking on the remaining three sides with cover being provided at the South End and on the West Side. The club's tenure in the Football League was brief, with it resigning its membership at the end of the 1922/23 season. Subsequently the Main Stand has been extended but remains substantially that constructed before admission to the League. Today, Bower Fold is still home to Stalybridge Celtic with the team currently playing in Nationwide North.

c1950s SYGE6

Burnden Park

Bolton Wanderers had already been a League team for seven years when the club moved to Burnden Park in 1895. The ground was destined to host League football for more than a century before the club relocated to the new Reebok Stadium for the start of the 1997/98 season. When first occupied, the ground was provided with an oval cycle track, the effect of which can be seen clearly by the shape of the open terrace at the north end — the Railway End Terrace — of the ground in this 1971 view. Other facilities in 1895 included a small stand on the east side. In 1904 a new West Stand was constructed to be followed in 1906 by the provision of covered terracing of the Great Lever (South) End. In 1915 a short angled extension to the West Stand to the south was constructed, and, in 1928, the construction of the Burnden Stand on the east, replacing the earlier structure. On 9 March 1946, 33 fans were killed and 400 injured during an FA Cup match against Stoke City when fans in the Railway End Terrace were crushed. As illustrated here, the ground remained largely unchanged until relocation; the only significant alteration occurred in 1986 when part of the Railway End Terrace was sold for development as a supermarket. Since the final match played at the ground, on 25 April 1997, the site has been redeveloped for retailing.
20 September 1971 A216922

27

County Ground

This view of Northampton Town's original ground shows well the essential problem that the club faced in sharing accommodation with the county's cricket team. Although the ground opened originally in 1885, it was not until 1897 that the football club first used the site. The facilities provided for football were limited: a small stand and terrace was constructed eventually on the north side in 1907. The Main Stand was rebuilt in 1924, shortly after the club was admitted to the Football League as a founder member of

Division Three in 1920, and again in 1930 after a fire; this was refurbished in 1980 but condemned after the Bradford fire of 1985 and partially demolished. Terraces were constructed at both the East and West ends; the West (Hotel) End was provided with a cover in 1951 and, following the club's promotion to the old First Division in May 1962, the terrace at the East End was extended. This is the position shown in this 1974 photograph. By the early 1990s, the club was in serious straits and in March 1992 went into Administration. Only the failure of Kidderminster Harriers to meet League standards kept Town in the League in 1993/94 but that was to be club's last full season at the County Ground; it relocated to the new Sixfields Stadium in October 1994. Today Northamptonshire County Cricket Club continues to occupy the venue.

25 January 1974 AC273084

Dean Court

Although technically not a lost ground as Bournemouth still plays on the site, the radical changes wrought at Dean Court qualify for entry into this book. Known as AFC Bournemouth since 1971, the club was founded in 1890 moving to Dean Court some 20 years later, playing its first game on the ground on 31 December 1910. The ground was built on the site of a former gravel pit and initially facilities were somewhat basic including a small 300-seat stand. With the team — then known as Bournemouth & Boscombe Athletic — elected as a member of Football League for the start of the 1923/24 season as a member of Third Division (S), the ground underwent considerable development. A 3,700 Main Stand was constructed in 1927 on the east side using material salvaged from the Empire Exhibition at Wembley and, in 1936, a covered terrace was constructed over the south end. The West Terrace was completely covered in 1957 and floodlighting was installed in 1961. The final major development at the original Dean Court occurred in 1992 when the Main (East) Stand was reclad. This is the condition in which the ground was photographed. For some years the club had been planning on relocation but, eventually, decided to rebuild Dean court completely. The work included the rotation of the pitch by 90 degrees and the construction of three stands. The team played its last game at the old ground on 28 April 2001 and its first at the new Fitness First Stadium on 10 November 2001; as a result of work not being completed for the start of the 2001/02 season, the club played its initial home games that campaign at the Avenue Stadium of Dorchester Town.
4 November 1992 616265

Drill Field

One of the most historic grounds in the British Isles, the Drill Field was home to Northwich Victoria for more than 125 years, although it only played host to League football for two seasons between September 1892 and April 1894. Victoria moved to the Drill Field in the mid-1870s and, although facilities were initially rudimentary, by 1892 when the club became a founder member of Division Two, a small stand had been constructed on the east side (known as the Dane Bank). The club resigned its membership of the League in 1894 but was to remain at the Drill Field until 2002 when it relocated and, sadly, this historic ground has subsequently been redeveloped. At the time of its closure it was the world's oldest continuously used football ground. Subsequent to the club's short League tenure, there were improvements in the ground. After the end of World War 1 the Dane Bank Stand was relocated to the west — town — side of the ground and the Dane Bank was provided with a new cover in 1928. The photograph, taken looking southeastwards some 70 years after the club's presence in the League, shows the ground as it existed in the early 1960s. The Dane Bank, which was terraced, was reroofed in 1950 and again in 1959. The Bus Terminus (North) End was covered after the end of World War 2; this cover was to survive until the late 1980s when it was removed as a result of safety fears following the Bradford City fire. The Water Street (South) End was also covered, as shown in this photograph, but the cover was destroyed in a storm during the 1966/67 season. In 1968, four years after the date of the photograph, the Main Stand portrayed was demolished and rebuilt.

1 October 1964 A141289

Eastville

One of two league grounds to have hosted Bristol Rovers to be featured in this book, Eastville was home to the team nicknamed the Gasheads for obvious reasons given the location of the works on the left of this 1951 view from 1897 through to 1986 when the team relocated temporarily to Twerton Park in Bath. The view as illustrated here shows the ground looking from the southwest with the 1920-built 2,000-seat South Stand in the foreground and the later (1958-built) cover over the north side opposite. The two terraces of the ground were altered in 1931 when greyhound racing was introduced and it was in 1940 that the football club sold the freehold of the stadium to the greyhound company. The cover over the West Terrace was constructed in 1961. For a brief period in the 1970s, from 1977-79, speedway was also accommodated at the ground and following the football club's departure in 1986, greyhound racing continued for some years. However, the ground's condition deteriorated and after partial demolition the entire site was redeveloped in 2001.

25 July 1971 A209329

Overleaf:
1951 A38127

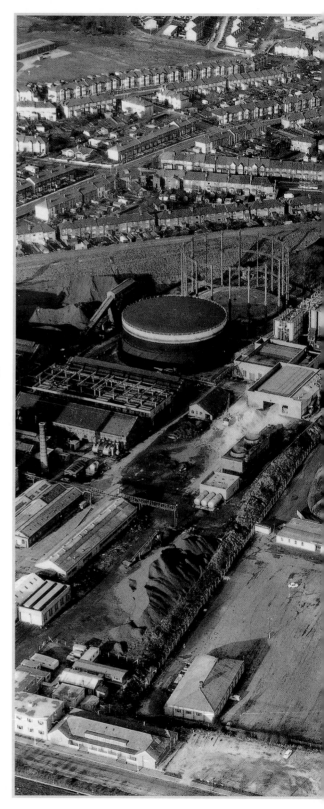

Elm Park

Reading first moved to Elm Park in 1896 and the club was to become a founder member of Division Three in 1920. Facilities originally provided included a stand on the north side. This was later supplemented by a cover over the northwest corner, but this and the Main Stand were destroyed in a gale in 1925. The ground as illustrated in the 1965 view taken looking towards the northeast shows the Main (North) Stand running along Norfolk Road; this had been constructed in 1926. Opposite in on the south is the Popular (Tilehurst Road) Side. The centre section of this side was covered in 1936 and the cover was extended towards the Town (East) End in the late 1940s and towards the West End in the mid-1950s. Elm Park was vacated by the team at the end of the 1997/98 season when the team relocated to the new Madejski Stadium. Today the site has been redeveloped for housing.
30 August 1965 A152103

Overleaf:
11 June 1968 A186123

Feethams

The saga of Darlington's relocation from Feethams to its new stadium on Neasham Road was complex and, ultimately, threatened the very survival of the club. In the event, however, the club survived, albeit under new ownership, and continues to play at the ground to which it moved at the start of the 2003/04 season. Feethams was the home of the club for more than a century. The cricket pitch was first established in the mid-1860s and, when Darlington FC was formed in 1883, the club moved to a site adjacent to the cricket field. The cricket pavilion, as shown in this view of both grounds looking to the north, was built in 1906. In terms of the football ground, the East Stand was built in 1919 and the West Stand two years later,

following the club's admission to the League as founder members of Division Three (N). The West Stand recorded in this 1972 photograph dates from 1961, the original structure having been destroyed by fire the previous year. Terracing was built at both the north (Cricket Field) and south ends; the former received a cantilevered roof in the late 1950s. The only significant change to affect Feethams before the club departed was the replacement of the East Stand; the new structure was constructed during 1998. Following the club's move to Neasham Road, Feethams was retained for use by the reserve and youth teams.

9 August 1972 A238917

Fellows Park

The home of Walsall for almost a century, the ground was initially known as Hillary Street when the club moved in during 1896. The name was not changed to Fellows Park until the 1930s. Walsall's League career began in 1896 when the club was elected to Division Two but this lasted only until 1901 when the club failed to be re-elected. A second League career commenced in 1921 when the club became a founder member of Division Three (N). The ground was relatively poorly developed for a number of years; in the 1920s the ground possessed a small Main (South) Stand and embankments on the remaining three sides (with the exception of the south-east corner where a laundry prevented development). Terraces were later constructed on the North (Popular) and West (Hillary Street) sides. In the early 1960s, as shown in the photograph, there had been a number of improvements and developments. The Hillary Street End was covered in 1965, at which time the old laundry was demolished and a narrow terrace constructed at the Railway (East) End. This was designed to be the paddock for a future East Stand, but this was never constructed. The final development, taking place in 1975, was an extension to the Main Stand. Walsall continued to occupy Fellows Park until the end of the 1989/90 season when the club relocated to the new Bescot Stadium. The old ground was subsequently demolished and the site used for a new supermarket.

12 September 1966 AV25264

Filbert Street

It was in 1891 that Leicester Fosse — the team became 'City' in 1919 — moved to Filbert Street and, three years later, the club was elected to membership of Division Two. The photograph shows the ground looking towards the north in 1971. The ground as illustrated here is very much the product of the post-World War 1 years. On 21 November 1921 the new Main (West) Stand was opened although the structure shown in the photograph was largely the result of rebuilding work in 1949 following damage during World War 2. The two-tiered South Stand, which replaced the Spion Kop, was opened on 26 November 1927; the existing cover over the South End was utilised to provide a cover for the Filbert Street (North) Terrace. The Popular (East) Side was covered during the 1930s and floodlighting initially installed in 1957. Seating was installed in the Filbert Street Terrace in 1971. In the years after the photograph, there were further changes, largely as a result of the need to convert the ground into an all-seater arena. In 1975 the roof of the North Stand was raised slightly to accommodate executive boxes and seats were fitted to the South Stand in 1994. The major change, however, came with the construction of a new 9,500-seat Main Stand; this cost £6 million and opened in December 1993. Despite this work, however, Filbert Street's capacity was only 21,500 and, in mid-1998, the club announced that it intended to relocate. The final game at Filbert Street occurred on 11 May 2002 before the club moved to the new Walkers Stadium. Filbert Street has subsequently been demolished and the site reused for residential purposes.
18 September 1971 A220594

47

Gay Meadow

One of three grounds to feature in this book for which the 2005/06 campaign will, in all probability, be their last, the Gay Meadow has been the home of Shrewsbury Town since 1910 when the club moved from The Barracks. However, the ground is some 20 years older than that, being used for football from late 1891. Shrewsbury Town first entered the Football League in 1950 when the team entered Division Three (N) when the number of League clubs was extended from 88 to 92. League status was retained for more than 50 years, until relegation to the Conference at the end of the 2002/03 season but was reclaimed, via the play offs, at the end of the following campaign. Located adjacent to the River Severn, the Gay Meadow was one of the most attractively located grounds in the country. The Main (West) Stand was built in three parts: the Centre Stand in 1922 and Station Stand before World War 2 — both were reroofed in 1966 when new offices were built behind the Centre Stand — and the Wakeman Stand. Opposite the Main Stand is the covered Riverside Terrace. The centre of this was covered between 1936 and 1939, the northern end in the 1950s and the southern end more recently. The ground also possessed open terraces at the Wakeman and Station ends, although the latter was partially covered between 1932 and 1937. Whilst the Gay Meadow is still in use at the time of writing, the site is likely to be sold for redevelopment as part of the funding scheme for the new ground and housing will probably be built on the site.

15 June 2004 697457

Goldstone Ground

The future Goldstone Ground was first used as a sporting venue in 1900 and, in 1901, Hove FC took over. At this stage a small stand was constructed at the south. In 1904 Hove FC was replaced by Brighton & Hove Albion, thus starting the club's 80-year association with the ground. By 1910 the ground had been further developed by the erection of a stand on the west. In 1920 Albion joined the League as a founder member of Division Three. The ground as illustrated in this 1972 photograph, taken looking towards the west, shows the covers on the South and North Ends; these had been covered in the 1930s. The Main (West) Stand had been constructed in 1958. Between 1979 and 1985 — the club was in the old Division One between 1979 and 1983 — a 974-seat temporary stand, nicknamed the Lego Stand, was constructed

between the West Stand and the North End. In 1979 the cover over the North End was removed; it was not replaced until 1985. In 1980 the South End was damaged by fire; it was repaired and seating installed. The East side was never covered; the club faced restrictions that precluded the construction of any structure taller than 50ft on the site. The Goldstone Ground was Albion's home until the end of the 1996/97 season, when it was forced to move out. Following two seasons sharing with Gillingham, the club returned to Brighton — and the Withdean Stadium — for the 1999/2000 season. The Goldstone Ground has been demolished and the site used for a retail development.

23 April 1972 A228235

Haig Avenue

Known as Ash Lane until 1921, when Southport was made a founder member of Division Three (N), Haig Avenue was initially provided with a timber North Stand when the club moved to the ground in 1905. The structure was extended when the club joined the League in 1921. The South (Popular) Side was provided with a cover at the same time. Known as the 'Scratching Shed', this was destined to last only to 1923, when it was replaced. This new structure was, however, only to last until early 1928. Between 1929 and 1931, covers were provided along the Scarisbrick New Road End and the Popular Side, leaving the Blowick Road End as an open terrace. The old Main Stand was destroyed by fire on 26 December 1966, and a new 2,000-seat structure, as illustrated in this 1971 view, was opened the following year. Southport's career as a Football League team came to an end at the end of the 1977/78 season when the club failed to be re-elected, and was replaced by Wigan Athletic. Following the club's demotion to non-league status the ground has changed significantly, with the ground being largely rebuilt, apart from the Main Stand, between the late 1980s and 1993.

16 September 1971 A216140

Highfield Road

One of two historic grounds to disappear at the end of the 2004/05 season, Highfield Road was the home of Coventry City for more than a century. The club first moved to the ground in 1899, at which stage the facilities were primarily a 2,000-seat South Stand. A second stand, on the Thackhall Street (North) Side was constructed in 1910 and, in 1919, following the club's election to Division Two, a cover was installed over the West Terrace. The photograph, looking northwards, illustrates the ground as it existed in the late 1960s. On the south side is the then new Main Stand, which had been completed in 1968 to replace a stand built in 1936 to replace the original structure. The two-tier West Stand was completed in 1967; this replaced an earlier structure, acquired second hand from Twickenham, erected in 1927. The Thackhall Street (Sky Blue) Stand had been rebuilt in 1963/64; this structure was to have a relatively short life in this form, being reroofed in 1972. In 1969 the only open area was the Kop (East) Terrace, which had originally been built in 1922. This was to be replaced by a new East Stand in August 1994. Both the Main and Sky Blue stands were also reroofed at this time. However, in mid-1998, it was announced that the club intended to relocate in order to secure a greater capacity. Ironically, however, the move to the new ground comes a year after the club surrendered its top-flight status. Coventry City played its last League game at Highfield Road on 30 April 2005 and will move to its new ground at Foleshill for the start of the 2005/06 season. Highfield Road has been sold for redevelopment and will be demolished.
10 June 1969 A197386

54

Holker Street

Viewed looking towards the west in 1968, Holker Street had been the home of Barrow since 1909 and had been a League ground since the team had become founder members of League Division Three (N) in 1921. The Main (North) Stand was constructed in 1912 and this was later extended. The covered accommodation at the West (Gasworks) End had been erected in 1920, having been transferred from the South Side where it was replaced by a larger covered enclosure. The East (Holker street) End was covered after World War 2 at which time the roof over the West End was also replaced. The floodlights illustrated were acquired second-hand from Arsenal in 1963. The ground remained a League venue until 1972 when the club failed to be re-elected; it was replaced in the Football League by Hereford United. Shortly after relegation, the club decided to modify the ground to allow speedway — the experiment only lasted five years — but resulted in the demolition of the covered terracing at the West End and the resiting of the pitch to the west. In 1979 the pitch was restored to its original alignment. In 1990 the South Stand was rebuilt and named after Ray Wilkie, a former manager of the team and, four years later, the North Stand was demolished and later rebuilt. The ground is still the home of Barrow today with the club now playing in Nationwide North.
19 July 1968 A188112

Horsley Hill

In 1908 South Shields FC moved to Horsley Hill from the club's earlier ground at Stanhope Road. There was a limited facility at the site for use by a Rugby Union team, but these were extended before South Shields entered League Division Two in 1919. The work included the construction of terracing, an extension to the existing Main (South) Stand (which originally predated World War 1) and the provision of covered accommodation on both the North and East sides. The photograph is taken looking towards the north and shows well both the South Stand and covered North Side. The ground played host to League football until the end of the 1929/30 season, when the club relocated to Redheugh Park and was reformed as Gateshead. Horsley Hill continued to host football thereafter, and as witnessed in this view taken in 1932, was later to accommodate greyhound racing as well. The latter continued until after World War 2 and, when this ceased, the ground was demolished. The site is now occupied by housing, although a bowling alley initially replaced the stadium after greyhound racing had ceased.

3 October 1932 40667

Lea Bridge Stadium

In 1930 Clapton (now Leyton) Orient moved to the Lea Bridge Stadium from its earlier Millfields Road ground. By this date, the Lea Bridge Stadium, viewed here looking towards the south, was already in use as a speedway track and boasted a covered Main (South) Stand. However, the Football League was not

satisfied with the size of the pitch and Orient was forced to play two home games at Wembley whilst work was undertaken at the Lea Bridge Stadium. Later improvements saw the construction of a small covered stand on the East Side and concrete terracing around most, but not all, of the perimeter. Orient continued to play matches at the Lea Bridge Stadium until the end of the 1936/37 season when the club relocated to its current ground at Brisbane Road. Speedway continued at the Lea Bridge stadium until after World War 2; when this ceased, the ground was demolished and redeveloped.

1933 42089

Leeds Road

Founded in 1908, Huddersfield Town used Leeds Road from the start, becoming a League team in 1910 when it was elected a member of Division Two. The photograph, taken looking towards the north, portrays the ground as it existed in 1968. On the south side is the Main Stand; this was constructed in 1950-51 to replace a structure destroyed by fire on 2 April 1950. The original South Stand had dated to 1910 at which date the alignment of the pitch had been rotated 90 degrees. The roof over the Leeds Road (West) End was also replaced in 1950-51, replacing a structure initially installed in 1929. The Popular (North) Side was roofed in 1955, having been extensively upgraded and expanded in the 1930s and 1940s. The open East Terrace was never to be covered. Apart from providing a home to Huddersfield Town, Leeds Road also provide temporary accommodation to Bradford City during the 1985/86 season when the Bantams were forced to play home games away from Valley Parade as a result of the May 1985 fire. From the late 1980s onwards, Town contemplated relocation and, in August 1992, permission was granted to construct the new McAlpine (now Galpharm) Stadium. Town played its last game at Leeds Road on 30 April 1994, starting the 1994/95 season at its new home. Leeds Road was subsequently demolished and redeveloped as a DIY store.

9 September 1968 A189804

Maine Road

Home of Manchester City for exactly 80 years, from 1923, when the team — already a member of the Football League — moved from Hyde Road, to 2003 when the club relocated to the new City of Manchester Stadium. The photograph shows the ground in the late 1950s and is viewed looking towards the southeast, with the Main Stand in the foreground. Constructed on a disused clay pit, the initial facilities included a 10,000-seat Main (West) Stand and terracing on the remaining three sides. Prior to the outbreak of World War 2, the cover was extended over the southwest corner. The next development was the provision of a cover over the Kippax (East) Terrace in 1956. In 1971 the open Scoreboard (North) End was replaced by a new North Stand. The Main Stand was reroofed in 1982. In 1992 the old Platt Lane (South) Stand, covered originally in 1938, was demolished, to be replaced in March the following year by the new Umbro Stand. The final development at Maine Road occurred with the construction of the new Kippax Stand in 1995. Although there were plans to redevelop Maine Road in a style similar to the Kippax Stand in order to achieve a 45,000-seat ground, the construction of the City of Manchester Stadium, designed to host the 2002 Commonwealth Games, allowed the club the option of relocating. The curtain came down on Maine Road at the end of the 2002/03 season and, although there were proposals for alternative sporting uses (including the possibility of Stockport County taking over), none of these schemes came to fruition and the ground has been demolished.
August 1959 AV11823

Manor Ground

A pre-existing sports ground when Headington United — Oxford United from 1960 — moved there in 1925, the Manor Ground was to survive until the end of the 2000/01 stadium when the long-planned move to the new Kassam Stadium was finally completed. The Main (West) Stand, which was some 50yd in length, was built in 1955-57 to replace facilities in the small stand, built in 1949, in the northwest corner. Oxford United was elected to the Football League in 1962 in replacement of the failed Accrington Stanley and the wedge-shaped Cuckoo (North) End, built in 1962-65, was built as a result of admission to the League. In 1963 the terracing at the London Road (South) End was covered and new floodlighting installed. For the 1984/85 season, which saw United progress to the old Division One, the two small stands on the Osler Road (East) Side were completed as was the provision of a new cover for the existing terrace on that side. The ground's small capacity — less than 10,000 of which only 60% was seated — and the constrained site meant that relocation was likely and, in mid-1995, it was announced that the club intended to build a new stadium. The photograph, taken looking towards the southeast, shows clearly the tripartite roof on the east side, the covered terrace at the south, the Main Stand on the west (with the open terrace beyond) and the open terrace at the north. In the event, delays ensured that the Manor Ground was reprieved until the 2000/01 season with its last game being on 1 May 2001. The site of the ground has subsequently been developed for housing and as part of a hospital.

5 September 1992 614429

Millfields Road

A member of the Football League since 1905, Clapton — later Leyton — Orient first played at Millfields Road in 1896. The ground had been used for whippet racing prior to the football club's arrival. The early facilities were rudimentary, comprising little more than four embankments and a covered press box. The next phase of development was the construction of a 2,000-seat South Stand in 1906; this structure was to be sold to Wimbledon in 1923 and re-erected at Plough Lane, at which stage a new stand was constructed.

The major development of the ground occurred after 1927 when greyhound racing, courtesy of the Clapton Stadium Syndicate, was introduced. The ground as illustrated in this photograph taken looking towards the 1923-built South Stand shows well the changes brought about by the arrival of the greyhounds: the rebuilt oval track; concrete terracing around the ground; and, increased covered accommodation. Orient's occupation, however, was drawing to a close and, on 3 May 1930, the club played its last match at the ground, relocating to the Lea Bridge Stadium for the 1930/31 season. Greyhound racing continued at Millfields Road for more than four decades. After closure, the site was cleared and used for housing.

4 August 1954 A55972

National Hockey Stadium

The story of the evolution of Wimbledon to Milton Keynes Dons is a long and tortuous one. Suffice to note here that, after some years based at Selhurst Park whilst seeking either to return to a ground in the London Borough of Merton or to relocate, the club moved to the National Hockey Stadium for the start of the 2003/04 season. However, it was always the intention that the club would move to its own purpose-built stadium and work on this commenced in early 2005 with the result that the team is scheduled to play the 2005/06 season at the National Hockey Stadium, prior to relocating for the start of the 2006/07 campaign. Thus this stadium is one of three scheduled to disappear from the footballing calendar this year, alongside Highbury and Gay Meadow. Dating originally from the early 1990s, with two main structures — a Main Stand on the south and a smaller stand on the north — the ground was expanded in 2003 prior to the arrival of the football club with two 'temporary' stands at the east and west ends, providing a total capacity of 9,000. Originally, these temporary structures were uncovered, but during the 2004/05 season, the stand at the east was fitted with a top cover. Planning permission for the construction of the new ground has been given with construction of the club's new 30,000 capacity stadium at Denbigh North commencing early in 2005; once the club relocates, the stadium will revert to being devoted solely to hockey and, in all probability, the temporary East and West stands will disappear.

25 May 2005 ADC698893

Northolme

Although recorded some years after Gainsborough Trinity played at Northolme, this venue played host to some 281 League matches between 1896 and 1912, when the club failed to be re-elected. The club was elected to the Second Division for the start of the 1896/97 season at which stage facilities were somewhat basic: players changed in a local pub. During the club's League career a small stand on the south was constructed — this was itself replaced in 1910 — and covered terracing on the north; both of these were destroyed by fire, as a result of vandalism, in the 1940s. The ground as illustrated in the photograph, taken looking northeastwards, shows the changes wrought over the past century. These include a new stand — the Victory Stand accommodating 300 — on the North Side (built in the 1940s) and the terraced enclosure at the Gasworks (West) End, dating from the 1930s. Northolme remains the home of Trinity at the time of writing.

24 October 1971 A220627

Odsal

On 11 May 1985 football was rocked by the fire at Valley Parade in which 56 spectators lost their lives. A day which should have been one of triumph for Bradford City — the club had just been awarded the old Third Division trophy was looking forward to Second Division football for the first time since before World War 2 — resulted in a scene of carnage. For the following season, whilst Valley Parade was rebuilt, City was forced to play its home games at Leeds Road (Huddersfield), Elland Road (Leeds) and Odsal, the home of Bradford Northern RLFC. A total of 21 league games were played at Odsal during the course of the 1985/86 season. The ground itself, constructed in the late 1920s, was home to Bradford Northern from 1934. A huge bowl, the ground had a nominal capacity of 150,000, although the maximum recorded was in May 1954 when almost 103,000 witnessed a Rugby League Challenge Cup Final replay; City's highest gate at the ground was, however, a more modest 13,831. Despite its scale, Odsal possessed only relatively rudimentary facilities, including covered accommodation only on the east and west sides. The 1976 view shows the ground very much as it existed throughout this period; it was only in the early years of the 21st century that agreement was concluded for the ground to be modernised for the now retitled Bradford Bulls. Apart from football and Rugby League, Odsal has also played host to a variety of other sports, including speedway, stock car racing and show jumping.

1976 314310

Old Recreation Ground

Located in Hanley, the Old Recreation Ground was home to Port Vale from 1913, when the club moved from its previous ground at Cobridge Athletic Ground, to 1950, when it moved to its current ground at Vale Park. The team was elected to League Division Two in October 1919 when Leeds City was expelled for making illegal payments to players. The facilities at the ground included the construction of the Main (West) Stand, concrete terracing and covered accommodation on both the east and north sides, all of

which are clearly visible in this view of the ground taken looking towards the east. The club owned the freehold of the site between 1927 and 1943, when it was resold to the local council. Following the club's move to Vale Park in 1950, the Old Recreation Ground was demolished and the site is today occupied by a multi-storey car park.

30 May 1937 53355

Old Show Ground

Although the Old Show Ground was home to a team based in the lower divisions, it can lay claim to one major innovation in the construction of football grounds: it was here, in 1958, that the first cantilevered stand roof was built in the British Isles. The future Scunthorpe United — known as Scunthorpe & Lindsey United until 1955 — was based at the Old Show Ground from its formation in 1910, although earlier clubs had used the site from the end of the 19th century. Initially, a Main (West) Stand was constructed; this was replaced in 1925 following a fire. Also visible in this view from 1988, taken with west towards the top, are the cantilevered East Stand of 1958 (replacing an earlier structure), the covered Doncaster Road (South) End (constructed in 1954) and the covered Fox Street (North) End (this was undertaken in 1959 and replaced a cover originally constructed in 1938). Floodlighting was installed in 1957. The club played its last game at the Old Show Ground on 18 May 1988 prior to starting the 1988/89 season at the new Glanford Park stadium. The Old Show Ground was subsequently demolished and the site used for a retail development.
1983 448667

Park Avenue

In 1907 Bradford (Park Avenue) FC was established and was admitted to League Division Two for the start of the 1908/09 season. There was already a ground at Park Avenue by this date with the northern part providing a football pitch and the southern being utilised for cricket. A new main stand, designed by the great Archibald Leitch, was constructed on the south side; this stand was double-sided, being used to provide covered accommodation for both the cricket and football supporters. The photograph, taken looking towards the southeast shows a game in progress towards the end of the 1965/66 season and shows well the Leitch designed stand. Covered accommodation was also provided on the north side. Concrete terracing was provided at both ends and a cover was also provided at the west end. In 1970, the club failed to gain re-election to the Football League — it had applied successfully in each of the previous three seasons — to be replaced by Cambridge United and dropped into the Northern Premier League. It continued to play at Park Avenue for a couple of seasons before playing one final season at Valley Parade. The club folded in 1973 but was subsequently reformed and is now playing in the Unibond Premier Division (having been relegated from Conference North at the end of the 2004/05 season). After the club left Park Avenue, the ground remained in increasing dereliction; cricket continued to be played at the adjacent cricket ground. Subsequently, the Main Stand was demolished and Yorkshire County Cricket Club built an indoor cricket school on part of the site. Elsewhere, however, much of the old ground remains derelict.

7 May 1966 A161355

Peel Croft

Although Burton upon Trent now possesses, in Burton Albion, a team vying to gain League entry through the Nationwide Conference, a century ago the town had a League team for more than a decade. Burton Swifts FC acquired Peel Croft from the town's Rugby Union team in 1890 and played their first game there in September 1891 and played their first League game in September the following year as a founder member of Division Two. In 1901 Burton Swifts, having finished bottom of Division Two and thus having to seek re-election, merged with local rivals Burton Wanderers to become Burton United with the new team retaining League status. However, the club again finished bottom of Division Two in 1907 and this time, was not re-elected. The club folded in 1910. This was, however, not to be the end of Peel Croft as the site was reacquired by Burton RUFC who continue to play there. Although the photograph, taken in 1952, is much later than the era of League football, it does show the 1907-built 600-seat Main Stand, which was constructed to replace the pavilion constructed in 1891 and which had been destroyed by fire earlier in 1907.

10 June 1952 A44095

Peel Park

By the date of this photograph, Accrington Stanley — one of the founder members of League Division Three (N) in 1921 — was approaching the end of the club's 40-year League career. The club resigned its membership in March 1962 and, although it tried to reverse this move, the Football League refused and the club's record for the 1961/62 season was expunged from the record book. For the start of the 1962/63 season, Oxford United was voted to League membership. Peel Park was acquired for Stanley in 1919. Before entering the League in 1921 a stand had been erected on the southeast side. The photograph, taken looking towards the southeast, shows both the original stand as well as that installed in 1958 on the northwest side; this was acquired second-hand from the Aldershot Military Tattoo. Following demotion, the club continued to play non-league football until 1965. It has been subsequently reformed and currently plays in the Nationwide Conference but at a new location. Peel Park was demolished after the club's collapse although part of the site remains in use as a school playing field.

18 July 1961 A93614

Penydarren Park

Used as a sporting venue since it was opened in 1904, Penydarren Park became the home of Merthyr Tydfil when the club was established in 1908. It was at that stage that the football pitch was laid out surrounded by the running track. Facilities included a small wooden stand on the south and a covered enclosure on the north. Merthyr Tydfil were founder members of League Division Three in 1920 and survived for a decade until failing to gain re-election at the end of the 1929/30 season. Following its exit from the League, the club collapsed in 1934 although Penydarren Park remained as a sporting venue, regaining a football team in 1945 when a reformed Merthyr Tydfil was established. The ground is still the team's home in 2005. The photograph illustrates the ground in the late 1950s.

28 September 1959 A78933

Plough Lane

The home of Wimbledon FC, Plough Lane became a Football League ground in 1977 when the team was elected to membership of League Division Four to replace Workington Town, thus beginning one of the strangest stories in Football League history. The rise and fall of Wimbledon and its re-emergence as Milton Keynes Dons is outside the province of this book; suffice to note that the end of the 1990/91 season saw the team move to groundshare with Crystal Palace but with the expectations — sadly proved over-optimistic — that it would ultimately return to a new ground in the Merton area. The ground was first used for football in 1912 and by the early 1930s comprised stands on the north and south side (the latter being acquired second-hand from Clapton Orient's ground at Millfields Road in 1923), with banking at the west end and terracing at the east. The photograph shows the ground as it existed shortly after the club turned professional in 1965. As a result of the generosity of Sydney Black, the ground had undergone significant development during the late 1950s, during which time (in 1959) the club acquired the freehold of the site. This work included the construction of the Main (North) Stand in 1958, the building of the Sportsman Pub at the northwest corner, the construction of a cantilevered roof over the West Terrace in 1959 and the installation of floodlights in 1960. Following the club's relocation in 1991, Plough Lane continued in use for football for some years for reserve matches; however, this has now ceased and the ground was demolished in 2002 for redevelopment. This view, taken looking towards the southwest, also shows, in the foreground, Wimbledon Stadium, used for greyhound racing.
20 June 1965 A146992

Portland Park

Known originally as Station Road Ground, Portland Park has been the home of Ashington FC since 1909. The club was a founder member of League Division Three (N) in 1921 at which stage the ground possessed a 1,000-seat stand on the north, a stand which was refurbished for the club's entry into the League. Concrete terracing was also constructed at the same time. However, the club's League career was to be relatively short as it failed to be re-elected at the end of the 1928/29 season. The ground remains today in use by Ashington although, as recorded in this 1981 photograph, it has undergone significant changes since League football was played here. The most notable were the result of the introduction of greyhound racing after World War 2, including a slight relocation of the pitch to the north. A new North Stand was constructed (this was again to be rebuilt after a fire in 1971 to the structure shown in the photograph), with terracing extending the full length of the pitch. On the south side, covered terracing was also provided; this was reduced and reroofed in the early 1990s as a result of asbestos. In addition to football and greyhound racing, Portland Park has also played host to stock car racing and speedway.
1981 416962

Recreation Ground

Aldershot FC was established in 1926 and leased the Recreation Ground from the local council from the start. Located within a public park, the latter had to be closed on matchdays in order to enable the club to collect ticket money. The first game played at the ground was on 27 August 1927; within two years the ground boasted a stand on the south side. The club was elected to the Third Division (S) for the start of the 1932/33 season and, following this, the North Side was covered. Further developments occurred after the end of World War 2, with the East End being covered and, in 1952, floodlights were installed for the first time. In 1970 the North Stand was altered with the addition of improved changing facilities and seating. This is the condition in which the ground was recorded in the mid-1970s. However, Aldershot suffered financial problems and was wound up in March 1992 following withdrawal from Division Four on 26 March 1992. The club's results for that season were expunged from the records. Today the ground is still used by the now reformed Aldershot Town FC who are battling to regain League status in the Conference.
5 May 1975 310973

Roker Park

In the increasingly commercial nature of football sentiment has only a limited role and, over the past 20 years, many of the best-known homes of football have disappeared. One of these casualties was Roker Park, home to Sunderland for almost exactly 100 years. The club, having been elected a member of the Football League in 1890, moved to Roker Park for the start of the 1898/99 season. The photograph, taken looking towards the north, shows Roker Park as it existed immediately after its refurbishment for use in the 1966 World Cup. Closest to the camera is the Clock Stand. Built in 1936 to a design by Archibald Leitch, it replaced one of the original 1898 stands. Opposite the Clock Stand is the Main Stand. Again the work of Leitch, this was officially opened on 7 September 1929. This was also a replacement of a stand originally built in 1898. The covered Fulwell End had been extended in 1925 but was only provided with a cover for the 1966 World Cup. The open Roker End was terraced in 1911, again following designs by Archibald Leitch, but the rear section of the terracing was dismantled in 1982. The decision to relocate from Roker Park was taken as a result of the necessity to convert the ground into an all-seater ground. Work started on the new Stadium of Light in 1996 and Sunderland bade farewell to Roker Park on 3 May 1997. The old ground was subsequently demolished and the site used for housing.

12 August 1968 A189987

Sealand Road

Chester moved to Sealand Road in 1906 and this was to be the club's home until the club moved to ground-share with Macclesfield Town at Moss Rose in 1990, as a result of financial difficulties, before the opening of the new Deva (now Saunders Honda) Stadium two years later. The club was admitted to the Football League in 1931 as a member of Division Three (N). The view taken here shows the ground as it existed in the early 1960s looking to the north. Visible are the Main (West Stand) constructed in 1931 when Chester joined the League, the covered Sealand Road Terrace (known as the 'Barn') and the part covered Popular Side on the east. Subsequent work saw the cover over the Popular (East) Side extended in 1968 and the construction of a new Main Stand in 1979. The team acquired the suffix 'City' in 1983. Following the club's departure in 1990, the new Main Stand was sold to Port Vale in 1992 and the entire site has now been redeveloped. Also as much a part of history as Sealand Road is the city's greyhound stadium, visible to the west of the football ground in this view.
1964 A128707

Seedhill

Nelson was a founder member of League Division Three (North) in 1921 but the club had been based at Seedhill since 1889 when it shared part of the cricket field to the north. In 1905 the club acquired the recreation ground to the south of the cricket field and a new ground was laid out. As illustrated in this 1925 photograph, taken looking northwestwards, the ground possesses a covered terrace on the North Side, a 1,500-seat stand on the South Side, which replaced a smaller structure constructed in 1905, and a covered West End. Much of this work had been taken contemporaneously with the club's admission to the Football League. At the end of the 1930/31 season, the club failed to be re-elected and thus fell out of the League; it did, however, continue in existence, playing at Seedhill until relocating to Victoria Park in 1970. The ground was then used briefly for stock car racing until the end of the decade when part of the site was acquired for use in the construction of the M65.
17 June 1925 13368

Somerton Park

The home of Newport County for more than 70 years, Somerton Park was first used by the team on its formation in 1912. The club was first admitted as a founder member of Division Three in 1920 but failed to be re-elected at the end of the 1930/31 season. In 1931 the ground passed into the ownership of the Cardiff Arms Park Greyhound Racing Co; by this date it possessed a Main (West) Stand and a covered end at the south. Further changes were required to accommodate greyhound racing: a new East (Main) Stand was constructed and the old West Stand modified into a social club. Newport County was readmitted to Division Three (S) at the start of the 1932/33 season and was to retain its League status until relegated to the Conference at the end of the 1987/88 campaign. The club folded shortly afterwards although it has been subsequently reborn. The ground, which had been through various ownership by the 1980s, was demolished in 1993 and the site is now occupied by housing. The photograph records Somerton Park as it existed in the mid-1960s; by this date speedway was also on offer at the venue. The photograph, taken looking towards the southwest, shows to good effect the track around the pitch, the covered South End and West Stand and the East Stand, nearest the camera, constructed when the ground was converted for greyhound racing.
16 August 1966 A165078

Southend Stadium

The home of Southend United for some 20 years, Southend Stadium was opened in 1934 with the club moving there from its earlier ground at The Kursaal. The ground, as is evident from its shape, was designed to serve both football and greyhound racing. It remained the home of United until the club relocated in 1955 to its current home at Roots Hall. The stadium continued to host greyhound racing until complete closure in 1985. It has subsequently been demolished and redeveloped as part of a shopping centre. Although the photograph, viewed looking northwards, was taken shortly after the stadium ceased to be used for football, it shows clearly the Main (West) Stand and covered East Side.
1 March 1963 A108403

Springfield Park

Originally opened in August 1897, Springfield Park in unusual in having played host to two Football League teams. As can be seen from the shape of the ground in this 1972 view, taken looking from the south, the ground was one of a number constructed in part to accommodate athletics, with a football pitch surrounded by a running track. In 1920, the ground became the home of the newly formed Wigan Borough, a club which was to become a founder member of League Division Three (N) on its creation for the start of the 1921/22 season. During the 1920s, a 2,000-seat Main Stand was built on the south side, but this was destroyed by fire in May 1953 and replaced the following year by the structure illustrated in the photograph. Also installed in the 1920s were covers over the North (Popular) Side and to the rear of the Shevington (West) End. However, Wigan Borough's League career was destined to be short and the club resigned from the League on 26 October 1931. The original club having collapsed, the ground was bought by Wigan Athletic. In 1978, Athletic became a member of League Division Four as a replacement for Southport, who had failed to be re-elected. The only significant change to Springfield Park during the years subsequent to the date of the photograph occurred later in 1972 with the replacement of the cover at the West End, although this was also later removed. Under the ambitious chairmanship of Dave Whelan, the club relocated to the JJB Stadium for the start of the 1999/2000 season, having played its last match at Springfield Park on 15 May 1999. The ground was subsequently demolished and redeveloped for housing.

24 March 1972 A223461

The Dell

First used by Southampton in 1898, when the club moved from its earlier ground, the County Ground, The Dell was to be home to the Saints for over a century, until the club relocated to the new St Mary's Stadium for the start of the 2001/02 season. The Dell became home to a League football team in 1920 when Southampton became a member of Division Three. The view here, taken in 1973, emphasises how confined the site was and how the club endeavoured to try and increase capacity. The photograph, taken looking towards the east, shows the West Stand, which dated to 1928. This was designed by Archibald Leitch to replace an earlier structure. Opposite is the East Stand; this structure was built in 1929 and was designed to replace one destroyed by fire on 4 May 1929. On the south side is the Milton Road End; shortly after World War 2 the club constructed three platforms at this end. These platforms, which were known as the 'Chocolate Boxes' were unique in English football as providing the only open upper-tier terraces. These platforms were demolished in 1981 but it was to be 1994 before the construction of the covered Milton Road Stand. On the north side, in 1973, was the open Archers Road End; in 1993, this too was to be rebuilt as a covered stand as part of the policy of converting The Dell into an all-seater stadium. However, the ground's limited capacity meant that the club was at a disadvantage within the Premier League and the decision was taken to relocate. The Dell played host to its final match on 19 May 2001 and has subsequently been redeveloped for housing.

5 September 1973 269650

The Den

Home to Millwall from 1910, when the club moved south of the river from its previous home at North Greenwich, The Den played host to League football from 1920, when the club became a founder member of Division Three, to 1993, when the club relocated to the New Den. The facilities in 1910 comprised an Archibald Leitch-designed Main Stand on the south and three open terraces. These open terraces were to

be covered during the 1930s, but the ground was to suffer serious damage in 1943 when a German bomb caused the destruction of the cover over the North Terrace and a cigarette caused the original Main Stand to be severely damaged by fire. The photograph, taken looking southeastwards, records the ground shortly after it had played host to its final game but before the demolition contractors moved it. The Main (South) Stand was reroofed in 1962 and fitted with seats. The last significant change occurred in 1985 with the extension of the cover on the North Terrace to provide a new family section. After the club's departure, the site was cleared and used for housing.

17 June 1993 620290

The Nest

Located to the east of Rosary Road and constructed in a former chalk pit, The Nest was the home of Norwich City from 1908 until the club moved to Carrow Road in 1935. This view, taken looking towards the north shows the ground shortly after the end of its career as a League venue in the late 1930s. Not well illustrated here, but an essential facet of the ground was the near precipitous cliff face at the east end of the ground, which provided very limited accommodation. Other facilities included stands along the two sides of the ground, which were moved to The Nest from the club's previous ground at Newmarket Road. The Nest became a League venue from the start of the 1920/21 season when Norwich City became a founder member of Division Three. After the club relocated in 1935 the ground was redeveloped as an industrial estate.

September 1937 SV8180 (part)

Tower Athletic Ground

Constructed as part of a leisure complex in the late 19th century, the Tower Athletic Ground played host to League football on two occasions: between 1898 and 1900 when it was the home of New Brighton Tower and between 1946 and 1951 when New Brighton played there. In this view, taken in 1946 shortly before New Brighton's five-year occupation, the ornate building on the extreme right was once the base for the tower; reminiscent of that constructed at Blackpool, the New Brighton version was demolished in the 1920s. New Brighton Tower was formed by the New Brighton Tower Company and, as can be seen, the pitch was surrounded by both a cycle track and running track. The facilities provided at this stage included

stands, with seated accommodation, on both the North and South sides. New Brighton Tower was elected to League Division Two in 1898 and resigned its membership two years later. By the outbreak of World War 2 the ground was largely decayed, a situation that worsened during the war, and the photograph shows well the decayed state of the ground before it was revamped for the start of the 1946/47 season when New Brighton moved here from Sandheys Park. These improvements included the construction of a new South Stand and remedial work on the West Terrace. At the end of the 1950/51 season, New Brighton failed to be re-elected to the League. Forced to abandon the ground in 1954, in 1955 the club returned in joint occupation with Wallasey Borough FC. New Brighton acquired the freehold of the ground in 1958 and continued playing there until 1977 when the site was sold for housing.

11 July 1946 A1713

Twerton Park

Temporary home to Bristol Rovers for a decade when the club departed from Eastville, Twerton Park was and is the home of Bath City (and has been since the early 1930s). The photograph, taken looking towards the north, shows the Main (North) Stand clearly; this was the structure constructed in replacement of that destroyed by fire in 1990. To the west of the Main Stand is the small Family Stand. Opposite the Main Stand is the covered Popular Side; this was initially provided with a cover in the 1930s but the present structure dates from replacement in the 1950s. The two open end terraces were originally embankments constructed out of the spoil resulting from the creation of the pitch from the hillside (a process that took some three years when the ground was constructed in the early 1930s); the terraces were concreted over in the 1950s. After the fire largely destroyed the original 1930s-built Main Stand, a temporary stand was constructed at the Bristol (West) End of the ground but this had disappeared by the date of this photograph. Bristol Rovers played its first game at the ground on 30 August 1986 and its last almost exactly 10 years later, on 17 August 1996, before relocating back to Bristol to groundshare with Bristol RUFC at the Memorial Ground. Twerton Park continues to be Bath City's home.

23 September 1992 614854

Vetch Field

The second of two historic grounds to disappear with the end of the 2004/05 season, the Vetch Field has played host to Swansea City (Town until 1970) since 1912. The club became a founder member of League Division Three in 1920. The photograph shows the ground as it existed in 1959 and views the ground looking to the west. The original part of the South Stand dates to 1913; it was subsequently extended to link up with the West Stand. This structure — at the Richardson Street End — was constructed in 1927. The North Bank was extended in 1925 and was provided with a cover in 1958, and so would have been virtually brand new when recorded here. In the years subsequent to the photograph the ground was modified. A new East Stand was opened in January 1982; this was curved towards the North Side and a one stage the club hoped to rebuild this side. These plans, however, failed to progress. In 1985 the upper tier of the West stand was closed and, in 1990, rather than demolish the structure, a new roof enclosing the upper tier was built. For some years, City's plans involved relocation. After some delay, the club started the new 2005/06 season at its replacement home, the New Stadium, with the last game being played at the Vetch Field on 30 April 2005.

1 September 1959 A78439

Victoria Ground

The home of Stoke City for more than 110 years, the Victoria Ground first played host to Stoke — it didn't acquire the suffix 'City' until 1925 — in 1883. The club became a member of League Division Two in 1919. The club has had three spells — 1888-1890 and 1891-1908 and from 1919 — in the League. The football pitch was originally located within a running track and early facilities included a 1,000-seat stand on the west side; this was replaced in 1922 and again between 1960 and 1963. The running track was removed in 1930 and this allowed for the construction of expanded terraces at the Boothen (South) End,

which was provided with a cover; at the time when the ground closed in 1997 this was the largest remaining terrace in English football. A 5,000-seat Butler Street (East) Stand was built with covers extending over the corners in 1935/36; this roof was destroyed by a gale in 1976 — shortly after this 1972 view taken looking towards the east — and replaced. The cover over the corner between the Butler Street Stand and Boothen End was removed in 1983 and the section of terracing abandoned. The two-tiered Stoke (North) End Stand was constructed in 1979; this was the final development of the Victoria Ground. In March 1986 permission was granted for the construction of the new Britannia Stadium and the final League game was played at the Victoria Ground on 4 May 1997. The site has subsequently been demolished.

29 June 1972 A242882

Watling Street

Although the home of Dartford from 1921, it was not until 1988 that Watling Street became a League ground when Maidstone United moved here to ground-share from their original Athletic Ground following admission to the Football League. The ground as portrayed in this photograph, which is taken looking eastwards, antedates slightly Maidstone's arrival but illustrates well the 1,000-seat Main Stand constructed in 1926 to replace an earlier structure destroyed by fire and the covered enclosure constructed in 1930 on the East Side. The only significant modification made to the ground prior to Maidstone's arrival was the construction of additional terracing at the south end. Maidstone's presence at Watling Street proved disastrous both for the guests and for Dartford; when Maidstone folded at the end of the 1991/92 season, Dartford also struggled and were forced to vacate the ground. The site was soon sold and was quickly redeveloped for housing.

1979 385974

Wembley

Pictured in October 1930, the old Wembley Stadium had a brief career as a venue for League football as Clapton Orient played two games on the hallowed turf in November 1930 as the pitch at its own Lea Bridge Stadium was deemed to be too narrow. In addition to these two matches, Wembley was also the venue for the various divisional Play-Off finals from their introduction at the end of the 1989/90 season through to the summer of 2000. Viewed looking to the northeast, this photograph demonstrates well the

facilities offered to fans of Orient and the two away teams — Brentford and Southend United — at the time, although the ground's capacity was hardly stretched: a total of 12,800 watched the two games. As can be seen, the ground was oval with a running track surrounding the pitch; covered accommodation was provided on the North and South sides. By the time the ground came to be used for Play-Off finals, the ground had been completely covered, in 1963, and converted to all-seater, in 1980, with the addition of a third tier of seating. However, as an all-seater stadium, Wembley was inadequate, particularly for those sitting at the lowest level, and, after much delay, work commenced in 2003 on the reconstruction of the ground. The new Wembley Stadium is scheduled for completion in time for the 2006 FA Cup final.

9 October 1930 34580

West Ham Stadium

Paradoxically not the home of West Ham United but of Thames FC, the West Ham Stadium was completed in 1928 and, with a notional capacity of some 120,000, was one of the largest grounds constructed in the United Kingdom. In footballing terms, however, it never justified this capacity as, during its short League career, Thames never achieved a gate of more than 8,275. The ground as built was

designed to accommodate both speedway and greyhound racing as well as football and was provided with covered seating accommodation on both sides and covered terracing at the north. Thames was admitted to Division Three (S) in 1930 but folded at the end of the 1931/32 season and did not seek re-election. As a greyhound and speedway stadium, the ground remained until the 1970s. It was subsequently demolished and the site utilised for housing. The view taken here shows the ground in 1928 shortly after its completion.

1928 24264

White City

Built for the Olympic Games of 1908, the White City Stadium played host to League football on two occasions when Queens Park Rangers were tenants of the Greyhound Racing Association (who had acquired the stadium in 1930). Although QPR had first played football at the stadium in 1912 when the club was in the Southern League, by 1931 QPR had been admitted to the League and the club played its first League match at the ground on 5 September 1931. The photograph, taken in 1931, is contemporary with this first spell as a League club at White City. It shows clearly the covered terraces constructed following the GRA's acquisition of the stadium; at this stage the ground's capacity was 80,000 but the

photograph also makes clear that, whilst the White City Stadium had better facilities and a greater capacity than Loftus Road, the distance from the pitch and the low attendances achieved meant that the atmosphere was poor. As a result, the club reverted to Loftus Road at the end of the 1931/32 season. Thirty years later, in 1962/63, QPR again played its home matches at White City; by this date the stadium had been fully covered and there were some 11,000 seats within the total capacity of 60,000. Again, however, the experiment proved unsuccessful and the club played its last match at White City on 22 May 1963. Although football was still to be played at the stadium — including the World Cup of 1966 — this was to be the end of White City in terms of League football. White City, however, continued to provide a home for greyhound racing, speedway and athletics before its final closure in 1984. The site was subsequently demolished and used for the expansion of BBC facilities.

1931 36467

Index of Clubs

Aberdare Athletic 12	Milton Keynes Dons 70
Accrington Stanley 84	Nelson 98
Aldershot 92	New Brighton Tower 112
Arsenal 10	New Brighton 112
Ashington 90	Newport County .100
Barrow 56	Northampton Town 28
Bolton Wanderers 26	Northwich Victoria 32
Bournemouth 30	Norwich City 110
Bradford City 62, 74	Oxford United 66
Bradford Park Avenue 80	Port Vale 76
Brighton & Hove Albion 50	Queens Park Rangers 126
Bristol Rovers 34, 36, 114	Reading 38, 40
Burton Swifts 82	Scunthorpe United 78
Burton United 82	Shrewsbury Town 48
Chester 96	South Shields 58
Clapton Orient 60, 68	Southampton 106
Coventry City .2, 54	Southend United 102
Darlington 42	Southport 52
Derby County .8, 16	Stalybridge Celtic 24
Gainsborough Trinity 72	Stoke City 118
Huddersfield Town 62	Sunderland 94
Hull City 18	Swansea City 116
Leicester City 46	Thames 124
Maidstone United 120	Walsall 44
Manchester City .64	Wigan Athletic 104
Merthyr Tydfil 86	Wigan Borough .104
Middlesbrough 14	Wimbledon 88
Millwall 108	Workington Town 22